GOD'S LITTLE INSTRUCTION BOOK *for* *African Americans*

Honor Books
Tulsa, Oklahoma

Text Compiled by June Brown, The Olive Oil Group,
Tulsa, Oklahoma 74134

Cover Credit: Reproduction from the original acrylic
on canvas signature image, "Sisters of Faith", created
for Faith Matters, Greensboro, NC. Copyright 2001
Synthia Saint James

3rd Printing

God's Little Instruction Book for
African Americans
ISBN # 1-56292-791-4
45-253-90012
Copyright © 2002 by Honor Books
P. O. Box 55388
Tulsa, Oklahoma 74155

Everything we have
or will be starts
out as potential.

"Before I formed you in the womb I knew you,
and before you were born I consecrated you;
I have appointed you a prophet to the nations."
Then I said, "Alas, Lord GOD!" . . . But the LORD
said to me, "Do not say, 'I am a youth,'
because everywhere I send you, you shall go,
and all that I command you, you shall speak.

Jeremiah 1:4-7 NASB

*A man who is afraid
of nothing in the discharge
of his duty, afraid of
no consequence personal
to himself, has his battle half
won before he strikes a blow.*

After Jesus said this, he looked toward
heaven and prayed: "Father, the time has come.
Glorify your Son, that your Son may glorify you.
I have brought you glory on earth by
completing the work you gave me to do.

John 17:1,4 NIV

*One with God
is a majority.*

What shall we then say to these things?
If God be for us, who can be against us?

Romans 8:31

The wise are as rare as eagles that fly high in the sky.

But they that wait upon the LORD shall renew *their* strength; they shall mount up with wings as eagles; they shall run, and not be weary; *and* they shall walk, and not faint.

Isaiah 40:31

A *man who has lost
everything but still has
God is a man who has
the potential to regain
what he has lost.*

Though he slay me, yet will I trust in him:
but I will maintain mine own ways before him.

Job 13:15-16

In trying to soothe
another's woes
Mine own had
passed away.

So in everything, do to others what you
would have them do to you, for this
sums up the Law and the Prophets.

Matthew 7:12 NIV

Believe in life!

Jesus saith unto him, I am the way,
the truth, and the life: no man cometh
unto the Father, but by me.

John 14:6

We must not allow anyone but God to assign our roles to us.

I know, O LORD, that a man's life is not his own; it is not for man to direct his steps.

Jeremiah 10:23 NIV

*It's an honor to be a father.
You may lose your hair
because of it, but it's an honor.
What hair you keep may
turn gray, but it's an honor.*

Fathers, do not provoke your children
to wrath, but bring them up in the
training and admonition of the Lord.

Ephesians 6:4 NKJV

*I am not going to die,
I'm going home like
a shooting star.*

There appeared a chariot of fire, and horses of fire, and parted them both asunder; and Elijah went up by a whirlwind into heaven.

2 Kings 2:11

Your dream will not come true until you make somebody else's dream or vision come true.

But ye *shall* not *be* so: but he that is greatest
among you, let him be as the younger;
and he that is chief, as he that doth serve.

Luke 22:26

*Don't look back.
Something might
be gaining on you.*

And Jesus said unto him, No man,
having put his hand to the plough, and
looking back, is fit for the kingdom of God.

Luke 9:62

*One universal Father
hath given being to us all;
And . . . we are all of the
same family, and stand in
the same relation to Him.*

Now you are no longer a slave but
God's own child. And since you are his child,
everything he has belongs to you.

Galatians 4:7 NLT

Social changes and social justice can be achieved by those of you who made the bold decision to apply your knowledge, your energy and your talent to humanitarian goals.

If it is encouraging, let him encourage;
if it is contributing to the needs of others,
let him give generously; if it is leadership,
let him govern diligently; if it is showing mercy,
let him do it cheerfully.

Romans 12:8 NIV

We must not continue to look over, around, through, or past those hurting around us.

We must help the weak, remembering
the words the Lord Jesus himself said:
'It is more blessed to give than to receive.'"

Acts 20:35 NIV

And I cried:
"Come back, my conscience;
I long to see thy face." But
Conscience cried: "I cannot;
Remorse sits in my place."

If we confess our sins, he is faithful
and just to forgive us *our* sins, and to
cleanse us from all unrighteousness.

1 John 1:9

If the society today allows wrongs to go unchallenged, the impression is created that those wrongs have the approval of the majority.

Can two walk together, except they be agreed?

Amos 3:3

No individual has any right to come into the world and go out of it without leaving behind him distinct and legitimate reasons for having passed through it.

For if you remain completely silent at this time, relief and deliverance will arise for the Jews from another place, but you and your father's house will perish. Yet who knows whether you have come to the kingdom for such a time as this?

Esther 4:14 NKJV

The color of the skin is in no way connected with strength of the mind or intellectual powers.

But the LORD said unto Samuel, Look not
on his countenance, or on the height of
his stature; because I have refused him:
for *the Lord seeth* not as man seeth;
for man looketh on the outward appearance,
but the LORD looketh on the heart.

I Samuel 16:7

God teaches humanity but one lesson concerning its duty to man and that is—Justice.

Give *instruction* to a wise *man*, and
he will be yet wiser: teach a just *man*,
and he will increase in learning.

Proverbs 9:9

*Oppression makes
a wise man mad.*

For oppression makes a wise man mad,
And a bribe corrupts the heart.

Ecclesiastes 7:7 NASB

The only reconstruction worthwhile is a reconstruction of thought.

And be not conformed to this world:
but be ye transformed by the renewing
of your mind, that ye may prove what *is* that
good, and acceptable, and perfect, will of God.

Romans 12:2

If prejudice could reason, it would dispel itself.

God hath shown me that I should not call any man common or unclean.

Acts 10:28

*Men get out of life
what they put into it,
but at an increased
rate of interest.*

Whatsoever a man soweth, that shall
he also reap. For he that soweth to his
flesh shall of the flesh reap corruption;
but he that soweth to the Spirit
shall of the Spirit reap life everlasting.

Galatians 6:7-8

*Don't confuse
wealth or fame
with character.*

A **GOOD** name *is* rather to be chosen
than great riches, *and* loving favour
rather than silver and gold.

Proverbs 22:1

*What the people
want is very simple.
They want an America
as good as its promise.*

That ye may be blameless and harmless,
the sons of God, without rebuke, in the
midst of a crooked and perverse nation,
among whom ye shine as lights in the world.

Philippians 2:15

Asking questions is not silly.

Pour out your heart before him:
God *is* a refuge for us.

Psalm 62:8

*Good actions
are nourishment
for youths, much
more than words.*

For as the body without the spirit is dead, so
faith without works is dead also.

James 2:26

*Have the courage of
your convictions.*

According to your faith be it unto you.

Matthew 9:29

A government which has power to tax a man in peace, draft him in war, should have power to defend his life in the hour of peril.

Hate the evil, and love the good, and establish judgment in the gate.

Amos 5:15

*Who listens to the voice
of the elderly is like a strong
tree; who turns a deaf ear
is like a twig in the wind.*

Hear, my son, and receive my sayings,
and the years of your life will be many.

Proverbs 4:10 NKJV

Power concedes nothing without a demand. It never did and it never will.

Then they were all amazed, so that they questioned among themselves, saying, "What is this? What new doctrine is this? For with authority He commands even the unclean spirits, and they obey Him."

Mark 1:27 NKJV

Equality is difficult, but superiority is painful.

For I say, through the grace given unto me, to every man that is among you, not to think *of himself* more highly than he ought to think; but to think soberly, according as God hath dealt to every man the measure of faith.

Romans 12:3

A person who cooperates according to undisciplined and unbridled emotions is like a cork bobbing on the water, constantly reacting to what other people do and say.

And they that are Christ's have crucified the flesh with the affections and lusts. If we live in the Spirit, let us also walk in the Spirit.

Galatians 5:24,25

Envy and pride are the leading lines to all the misery that mankind has suffered from the beginning of the world to this present day.

Then you say in your heart, "My power and the might of my hand have gained me this wealth." And you shall remember the LORD your God, for *it is* he who gives you power to get wealth.

Deuteronomy 8:17-18 NKJV

*It's a poor rule
that won't work
both ways.*

These also are sayings of the wise:
To show partiality in judging is not good.

Proverbs 24:23 NIV

Error moves with quick feet . . . and truth must never be lagging behind.

Gird thy sword upon thy thigh, O most mighty, with thy glory and thy majesty. And in thy majesty ride prosperously because of truth and meekness and righteousness; and thy right hand shall teach thee terrible things.

Psalm 45:3-5

To read without reflecting is to cram the intellect and paralyze the mind.

Consider your ways.

Haggai 1:5

In the fullness of time all things will end well.

Henceforth there is laid up for me a crown of righteousness, which the Lord, the righteous judge, shall give me at that day: and not to me only, but unto all them also that love his appearing.

2 Timothy 4:8

Hatred and bitterness can never cure the disease of fear; only love can do that.

Love is patient, love is kind. . . .
Love does not delight in evil but
rejoices with the truth. It always protects,
always trusts, always hopes, always perseveres.

1 Corinthians 13:4,6-7 NIV

The ruin of a nation begins in the homes of its people.

Never . . . forget what you have seen the
LORD do for you. Do not let these things
escape from your mind as long as you live!
And be sure to pass them on to your children
and grandchildren . . . That way, they will
learn to fear me as long as they live, and they
will be able to teach my laws to their children.

Deuteronomy 4:9-10 NLT

The atmosphere of homes is no rarer and purer and sweeter than are the mothers in those homes.

She stretcheth out her hand
to the poor; yea, she reacheth
forth her hands to the needy.

Proverbs 31:20

There are two kinds of everything, the genuine and the counterfeit. Morality claims only the genuine.

Not with eyeservice, as menpleasers; but as the servants of Christ, doing the will of God from the heart.

Ephesians 6:6

*Tell them that
the sacrifice was
not in vain.*

And they have defeated him
because of the blood of the Lamb
and because of their testimony.
And they were not afraid to die.

Revelations 12:11 NLT

*When a man gains a
clear vision, he comes
into a new understanding
of himself.*

And immediately there fell from his eyes
as it had been scales: and he received sight
forthwith, and arose, and was baptized.

Acts 9:18

It is only what is written upon the soul of man that will survive the wreck of time.

Keep thy heart with all diligence;
for out of it are the issues of life.

Proverbs 4:23

It is the indispensable duty of those, who maintain for themselves the rights of human nature, and who possess the obligations of Christianity, to extend their power and influence to the relief of every part of the human race.

Stop doing wrong, learn to do right! Seek justice, encourage the oppressed.

Isaiah 1:16-17 NIV

We work on the surface; the depths are a mystery.

For now we see through a glass, darkly;
but then face to face: now I know in part;
but then shall I know even as also I am known.

1 Corinthians 13:12

Righteousness and popularity are not always yoke-fellows, and sometimes run a contrary course.

Blessed *are* they which are
persecuted for righteousness' sake:
for theirs is the kingdom of heaven. . . .
Rejoice, and be exceeding glad:
for great *is* your reward in heaven.

Matthew 5:10,12

Let us seek
peace and
not confusion.

God is not *the author* of confusion,
but of peace, as in all churches of the saints.

I Corinthians 14:33

The wind does not break a tree that bends.

Therefore take up the whole armor of God, that you may be able to withstand in the evil day, and having done all, to stand.

Ephesians 6:13 NKJV

*No child is ever spoiled
by too much attention.
It is the lack of attention
that spoils.*

And whoso shall receive one such
little child in my name receiveth me.

Matthew 18:5

Who tells the truth is never wrong.

Sanctify them through thy truth:
thy word is truth.

John 17:17

The highest test of the civilization of any race is its willingness to extend a helping hand to the less fortunate.

For the poor shall never cease out of the land: therefore I command thee, saying, Thou shalt open thine hand wide unto thy brother, to thy poor, and to thy needy, in thy land.

Deuteronomy 15:11

*O God, give me
words to make my
dream-children live.*

He took him outside and said, "Look up at
the heavens and count the stars—if indeed you
can count them." Then he said to him, "So shall
your offspring be." Abram believed the LORD.

Genesis 15:5-6 NIV

If the first woman God ever made was strong enough to turn the world upside down all alone, . . . women together ought to be able to turn it back, and get it right side up again!

He giveth power to the faint; and to *them that have* no might he increaseth strength.

Isaiah 40:29

God done settled it dat one woman is enough fer a man, an' two is a war on yer hands.

A wife of noble character is her husband's crown, but a disgraceful wife is like decay in his bones.

Proverbs 12:4 NIV

Every man leaves his footprints.

O LORD, I know that the way of man
is not in himself: *it is* not in man
that walketh to direct his steps.

Jeremiah 10:23

*Education is a power
when rightly used, and
a curse when abused.*

When wisdom entereth into thine heart,
and knowledge is pleasant unto thy soul;
Discretion shall preserve thee,
understanding shall keep thee.

Proverbs 2:10-11

*Woman, Mother—your responsibility
is one that might make angels
tremble and fear to take hold.
To trifle with it, to ignore or misuse
it, is to treat lightly the most sacred
and solemn trust ever confided
by God to human kind.*

Who can find a virtuous wife? For her
worth *is* far above rubies. Her children
rise up and call her blessed; her husband
also, and he praises her: "Many daughters
have done well, but you excel them all."

Proverbs 31:10, 28-29 NKJV

*Sometimes I feel
like a motherless child,
A long way from home*

The Lord shall comfort Zion:
he will comfort all her waste places;
and he will make her wilderness like Eden,
and her desert like the garden of the LORD;
joy and gladness shall be found therein,
thanksgiving, and the voice of melody.

Isaiah 51:3

The Lord who told me to take care of my people meant me to do it just as long as I live, and so I do what he told me.

Blessed *is* she that believed: for there shall be a performance of those things which were told her from the LORD.

Luke 1:45

If a man wants to know his own strength, he need not measure himself. He needs only to size up the fellows who are pulling against him to find out how strong he is.

For we are not fighting against people made of flesh and blood, but against the evil rulers and authorities of the unseen world, against those mighty powers of darkness who rule this world, and against wicked spirits in the heavenly realms.

Ephesians 6:12 NLT

If there is no struggle, there is no progress.

Our struggle is not against flesh and blood, but against the rulers, against the authorities, against the powers of this dark world and against the spiritual forces of evil in the heavenly realms.

Ephesians 6:12 NIV

There is a difference between time and timing.

Let us not be weary in well doing: for in due season we shall reap, if we faint not.

Galatians 6:9

If we must die—oh, let us nobly die, so that our precious blood may not be shed in vain.

Holding forth the word of life; that I may rejoice in the day of Christ, that I have not run in vain, neither laboured in vain.

Philippians 2:16

You are invited to join the hunt when your nets are in evidence.

"Which of you, intending to build a tower, does not sit down first and count the cost, whether he has **enough** to finish it—lest, after he has laid the foundation, and is not able to finish it. . . . So likewise, whoever of you does not forsake all that he has cannot be My disciple."

Luke 14:28-30, 33 NKJV

*Drugs take you further
than you want to go.
Keep you longer than you want
to stay. And cost you more
than you can ever pay.*

And so, dear brothers and sisters, I plead
with you to give your bodies to God. Let them
be a living and holy sacrifice—the kind
he will accept. When you think of what he
has done for you, is this too much to ask?

Romans 12:1 NLT

Mental inertia is death.

The wise in heart will receive commandments:
but a prating fool shall fall.

Proverbs 10:8

Dear children, everything you do or say in life tells; tells upon souls; tells in all time; tells forever and ever.

"And to the angel of the church in Thyatira write, 'These things says the Son of God, . . . "I know your works, love, service, faith, and your patience; and as for your works, the last are more than the first.

Revelation 2:18-19 NKJV

When your neighbor is wrong you point a finger, but when you are wrong you hide.

Then you will call, and the LORD will answer; you will cry, and He will say, 'Here I am.' If you remove the yoke from your midst, the pointing of the finger, and speaking wickedness.

Isaiah 58:9 NASB

*Words cannot express
the exultation felt by the
individual as he finds himself,
with hundreds of his fellows,
behind prison bars for a
cause he knows is just.*

Shadrach, Meshach, and Abed-Nego answered and
said to the king, "O Nebuchadnezzar, we have
no need to answer you in this matter. If that
is the case, our God whom we serve is able
to deliver us from the burning fiery furnace,
and He will deliver us from your hand, O king.

Daniel 3:16-17 NKJV

I had faith in a living God, faith in myself, and a desire to serve.

O Sovereign LORD, you are God! Your words are trustworthy, and you have promised these good things to your servant.

2 Samuel 7:28 NIV

No word.
But there was
"hope".

Hope deferred maketh the heart sick: but
when the desire cometh, it is a tree of life.

Proverbs 13:12

*No matter how fast or loudly
you talk, no matter how skillfully
you present your case or repeat
your self-justifications, you are
headed for trouble if you choose
your way over His way.*

Hath the LORD *as great* delight
in burnt offerings and sacrifices,
as in obeying the voice of the Lord?
Behold to obey *is* better than sacrifice,
and to hearken than the fat of rams.

1 Samuel 15:22

Faith is an action; it is always moving.

For when we place our faith
in Christ Jesus. . . . What is important
is faith expressing itself in love.

Galatians 5:6 NLT

The future belongs
to the people.

Blessed *are* they that do his commandments,
that they may have right to the tree of life, and
may enter in through the gates into the city.

Revelations 22:14

I see the potential to make a difference. And I get the courage to break away from the crowd.

Be strong and of a good courage, fear not, nor be afraid of them: for the LORD thy God, he *it is* that doth go with thee; he will not fail thee, nor forsake thee.

Deuteronomy 31:6

Isn't God good?

And Jesus said unto him,
Why callest thou me good?
none *is* good, save one, *that is*, God.

Luke 18:19

Unforgiveness is a tombstone in the graveyard.

Let all bitterness, and wrath, and anger, and clamour, and evil speaking, be put away from you, . . . forgiving one another. . . .

Ephesians 4:31-32

Truth burns up error.

Every man's work shall be made manifest:
for the day shall declare it, because it shall
be revealed by fire; and the fire shall try
every man's work of what sort it is.

I Corinthians 3:13

When men sow the wind it is rational to expect that they will reap the whirlwind.

He that observeth the wind shall not sow; and he that regardeth the clouds shall not reap.

Ecclesiastes 11:4

Wishes pass with the moment. Dreams carry the weight of eternity.

The angel of the LORD appeared unto him in a dream, saying, Joseph, thou son of David, fear not to take unto thee Mary thy wife: for that which is conceived in her is of the Holy Ghost. And she shall bring forth a son, and thou shalt call his name JESUS: for he shall save his people from their sins.

Matthew 1:20-21

*Success is measured not
so much by the position
that one has reached in life,
as by the obstacles which
he has overcome.*

He that overcometh shall inherit all things;
and I will be his God, and he shall be my son.

Revelations 21:7

The present freedom and tranquility which you enjoy you have mercifully received, and . . . it is the peculiar blessing of Heaven.

The LORD turn his face toward you
and give you peace.

Numbers 6:26 NIV

There is more wisdom in listening than in speaking.

He who restrains his words has knowledge, and he who has a cool spirit is a man of understanding.

Proverbs 17:27 NASB

Reaching our God-given dreams is impossible to do alone, but we are not alone!

"For I know the plans I have for you," says the LORD. "They are plans for good and not for disaster, to give you a future and a hope. In those days when you pray, I will listen."

Jeremiah 29:11-12 NLT

*Peace is costly
but it is worth
the expense.*

But he *was* wounded for our transgressions,
he was bruised for our iniquities:
the chastisement of our peace *was* upon him;
and with his stripes we are healed.

Isaiah 53:5

A charitable man is the true lover of God.

If there be among you a poor man of one of thy brethren within any of thy gates in thy land which the LORD thy God giveth thee, thou shalt not harden thine heart, nor shut thine hand from thy poor brother.

Deuteronomy 15:7

*There is in this world
no such force as
the force of a man
determined to rise.*

Behold, the people shall rise up as a great
lion, and lift up himself as a young lion:
he shall not lie down until he eat of
the prey, and drink the blood of the slain.

Numbers 23:24

Don't sit down and wait for the opportunities to come: you have to get up and make them.

Have I not commanded you? Be strong and courageous. Do not be terrified; do not be discouraged, for the LORD your God will be with you wherever you go."

Joshua 1:9 NIV

To do the best one can, wherever placed, is a summary of all the rules of success.

This one thing I do, forgetting those things which are behind, and reaching forth unto those things which are before, I press toward the mark for the prize of the high calling of God in Christ Jesus.

Philippians 3:13-14

*As far as God is
concerned there are
no ugly people. . . .
We are all made in the
very likeness of God.*

So God created man in his own image,
in the image of God created he him;
male and female created he them.

Genesis 1:27

It is the mind that makes the body.

I will put my laws in their minds
and write them on their hearts.

Hebrews 8:10 NIV

One who damages
the character of
another damages
his own.

He that hideth hatred with lying lips,
and he that uttereth a slander, is a fool.

Proverbs 10:18

*Just be calm,
be brave and true,
Keep your head and
you'll get through.*

The disciples went and woke him, saying,
"Lord, save us! We're going to drown!" He replied,
"You of little faith, why are you so afraid?"
Then he got up and rebuked the winds and
the waves, and it was completely calm.

Matthew 8:25-26 NIV

*Real joy has little to do
with what's in your hand,
rather what's in your
heart and soul.*

But let all those that put their trust in
thee rejoice: let them ever shout for joy,
because thou defendest them: let them also
that love thy name be joyful in thee.

Psalm 5:11

*When our thoughts—
which bring actions—
are filled with hate
against anyone, . . .
we are in a living hell.*

But he who hates his brother is in
darkness and walks in darkness, and does
not know where he is going, because
the darkness has blinded his eyes.

1 John 2:11 NKJV

Without effort,
no harvest will
be abundant.

I went by the field of the slothful, and by the
vineyard of the man void of understanding;
And, lo, it was all grown over with thorns,
and nettles had covered the face thereof,
and the stone wall thereof was broken down.

Proverb 24:30-31

*A friend works in
the light of the sun,
an enemy in the dark.*

Faithful *are* the wounds of a friend; but
the kisses of an enemy *are* deceitful.

Proverbs 27:6

You cannot to your God attend, And serve the God of Mammon.

"No servant can serve two masters: for either he will hate the one, and love the other, or else he will hold to the one, and despise the other. Ye cannot serve God and mammon."

Luke 16:13

If you have a lot, give some of your possessions; if you have little, give some of your heart.

And though I bestow all my goods to feed *the poor*, and though I give my body to be burned, but have not love, it profits me nothing.

1 Corinthians 13:3 NKJV

Old Civilizations die hard, and old prejudices die harder.

The Samaritan woman said to him,
"You are a Jew and I am a Samaritan woman.
How can you ask me for a drink?"
(For Jews do not associate with Samaritans.)

John 4:9 NIV

To preach is not sufficient, as practice speaks much louder than words.

The Son of man came not to be ministered unto, but to minister, and to give his life a ransom for many.

Matthew 20:28

*God provides for
the blind vulture.*

Look at the birds of the air; they do
not sow or reap or store away in barns,
and yet your heavenly Father feeds them.
Are you not much more valuable than they?

Matthew 6:26 NIV

*Forgiveness is not
an occasional act:
it is a permanent
attitude*

And be ye kind one to another, tenderhearted,
forgiving one another, even as God
for Christ's sake hath forgiven you.

Ephesians 4:32

> # An undecided man is the worst disaster of the village.

A double minded man *is* unstable in all his ways.

James 1:8

*Who digs a well
should not be
refused water.*

For the Scripture says, *"You shall not
muzzle an ox while it treads out the grain,"*
and, "The laborer *is* worthy of his wages."

1 Timothy 5:18 NKJV

*Those who
waste time only
hurt themselves.*

See then that ye walk circumspectly, not as fools,
but as wise, redeeming the time.

Ephesians 5:15-16

*Let lessons of
stern yesterdays . . .
be your food, your
drink, your rest.*

It *is* good for me that I have been afflicted;
that I might learn thy statutes.

Psalms 119:71

*If you wash yourself
in anger you never
have clean hands.*

He who is quick-tempered acts foolishly,
And a man of wicked intentions is hated.

Proverbs 14:17 NKJV

We must accept finite disappointment, but we must never lose infinite hope.

But now, LORD, what do I look for?
My hope is in you.

Psalm 39:7 NIV

*A friend is
someone who
walks by your side.*

A man who has friends must himself
be friendly, but there is a friend
who sticks closer than a brother.

Proverbs 18:24 NKJV

*Evil communications
corrupt good manners.
I hope to live to hear that
good communications
correct bad manners.*

Let your conversation be always full
of grace, seasoned with salt, so that
you may know how to answer everyone.

Colossians 4:6 NIV

*Come, Liberty! Thou cheerful
sound, Roll through my
ravished ears; Come, let my
grief in joys be drowned,
And drive away my fears.*

I will rejoice and be glad in Thy lovingkindness,
because Thou hast seen my affliction;
Thou hast known the troubles of my soul.

Psalm 31:7 NASB

*When you need to make
an important decision,
never do it alone,
choose the right people.*

Where no counsel *is*, the people fall: but in
the multitude of counsellors *there is* safety.

Proverbs 11:14

When you receive a God-given dream, not a wish or a fantasy, God will give you the strength and courage to walk it out.

For a dream comes through much activity,
And a fool's voice is known by his many words.

Ecclesiastes 5:3 NKJV

Any honest appraisal of history reveals that most of the things suffered by mankind came about because someone somewhere chose to do things their way instead of God's way.

All we like sheep have gone astray; we have turned every one to his own way; and the LORD hath laid on him the iniquity of us all.

Isaiah 53:6

*The best time to
do a thing is when
it can be done.*

There is a time for everything, and a
season for every activity under heaven.

Ecclesiastes 3:1 NIV

*There is time enough,
but none to spare.*

Jesus therefore said to them,
"My time is not yet at hand, but
your time is always opportune.

John 7:6 NASB

*The rich man who achieves
a degree of greatness achieves
it not because he hoards
his wealth, but because
he gives it away in the
interest of good causes.*

It is possible to give freely and
become more wealthy, but those
who are stingy will lose everything.

Proverbs 11:24 NLT

The heart is a locket that does not open easily.

Counsel in the heart of man *is like* deep water;
but a man of understanding will draw it out.

Proverbs 20:5

*Believe in prayer.
It is the best way we
have to draw strength
from heaven.*

"If you believe, you will receive
whatever you ask for in prayer."

Matthew 21:22 NIV

*It is self-evident,
that when the greatest
difficulties surround us,
we should summon
our noblest powers.*

The LORD GOD is my strength; and
He will make my feet like deer's feet, and
He will make me walk on high hills.

Habakkuk 3:19 NKJV

Nature is an unlimited broadcasting station, . . . through which God speaks to us every hour, if we only tune in.

My heart has heard you say,
"Come and talk with me." And my heart
responds, "LORD, I am coming."

Psalm 27:8 NLT

On the dusty earth-drum
Beats the falling rain;
Now a whispered murmur,
Now a louder strain.

Behold, the LORD passed by, and a great
and strong wind rent the mountains . . . ;
but the LORD was not in the wind: and after
the wind an earthquake; but the LORD was
not in the earthquake: And after the earthquake
a fire; but the LORD was not in the fire:
and after the fire a still small voice.

1 King 19:11-12 NKJV

Lord, help me live from day to day, in such a self-forgotten way that when I kneel to pray, my prayer shall be for others.

Praying always with all prayer and supplication in the Spirit, and watching thereunto with all perseverance and supplication for all saints.

Philippians 6:18 NKJV

*Religion without
humanity is a
poor human stuff.*

Do nothing out of selfish ambition or
vain conceit, but in humility consider others
better than yourselves. Each of you should
look not only to your own interests,
but also to the interests of others.

Philippians 2:3-4 NIV

Don't pray when it rains if you don't pray when the sun shines.

Then Jesus told his disciples a parable
to show them that they should
always pray and not give up.

Luke 18:1 NIV

We often learn as much in life from examples of what "not to do" as we learn from examples of what "to do."

He did what was right in the eyes of the LORD, just as his father David had done.

2 Chronicles 29:2 NIV

*The amount of knowledge
that a man has does not
secure his usefulness if
he has so taken it in
that he is lop-sided.*

For wisdom *is* a defence, *and* money *is* a defence:
but the excellency of knowledge *is,*
that wisdom giveth life to them that have it.

Ecclesiastes 7:12

*I know why the caged bird sings, ah me,
When his wing is bruised and
his bosom sore, –
When he beats his bars and he
would be free;
It is not a carol of joy or glee,
But a prayer that he sends from
his heart's deep core.*

If I take the wings of the morning,
and dwell in the uttermost parts of the sea;
even there shall thy hand lead me,
and thy right hand shall hold me.

Psalms 139:9-10

A little learning, indeed, may be a dangerous thing, but the want of learning is a calamity to any people.

My people are destroyed for
lack of knowledge.

Hosea 4:6

Education must not simply teach work— it must teach life.

My son, give attention to my words; . . .
For they are life to those who find them,
And health to all their whole body.

Proverbs 4:20-22 NASB

*Train your head
and hands to do,
your head and
heart to dare.*

Be strong and of good courage, and
do *it*: fear not, nor be dismayed: for the
LORD God, even my God, will be with thee;
he will not fail thee, nor forsake thee.

1 Chronicles 28:20

Education is the key to unlock the golden door of freedom.

As your words are taught, they give light;
even the simple can understand them.

Psalm 119:130 NLT

*Our elevation must be the
result of self-efforts, and
work of our own hands.*

The sleep of a labouring man *is* sweet,
whether he eat little or much:
but the abundance of the rich
will not suffer him to sleep.

Ecclesiastes 5:12

Education means to inspire people to live more abundantly, to learn to begin with life as they find it and make it better.

For whoso findeth me [Wisdom] findeth life, and shall obtain favour of the LORD.

Proverbs 8:35

Strive to make something of yourself; then strive to make the most of yourself.

I know all the things you do—your love, your faith, your service and your patient endurance. And I can see your constant improvement in all these things.

Revelations 2:18-20 NLT

*Excellence is to
do a common thing
in an uncommon way.*

Seest thou a man diligent in his business?
he shall stand before kings;
he shall not stand before mean *men.*

Proverbs 22:29

Educate your sons and daughters, send them to school, and show them that beside the cartridge box, the ballot box, and the jury box, you have also the knowledge box.

Apply thine heart unto instruction, and thine ears to the words of knowledge

Proverbs 23:12

Hope is the pillar of the world

For I know the thoughts that I think toward you, says the LORD, thoughts of peace and not of evil, to give you a future and a hope. Then you will call upon Me and go and pray to Me, and I will listen to you. And you will seek Me and find Me, when you search for Me with all your heart.

Jeremiah 29:11-13 NKJV

Wisdom is higher than a fool can reach.

If any of you lack wisdom, let him ask of God, that giveth to all men liberally.

James 1:5

*With our short sight
we affect to take a
comprehensive view
of eternity. Our horizon
is the universe.*

Have you not known? Have you not heard?
The everlasting God, the LORD, The Creator
of the ends of the earth, Neither faints nor
is weary. His understanding is unsearchable

Isaiah 40:28 NKJV

*One needs occasionally
to stand aside from the
hum and rush of human
interests and pass on to
hear the voice of God.*

The Lord looked down from heaven upon
the children of men, to see if there were
any that did understand *and* seek God.

Psalm 14:2

It is not light that we need, but fire: it is not the gentle shower, but thunder. We need the storm, the whirlwind, and the earthquake.

Tremble, O earth, at the presence of the Lord,

Psalm 114:7 NIV

God is a God of order who is never "caught off-guard" by events or the actions of others.

Only I can tell you what is going to happen even before it happens. Everything I plan will come to pass.

Isaiah 46:10 NLT

*Pray with a
listening ear.*

And thine ears shall hear a word behind thee,
saying, This *is* the way, walk ye in it,
when ye turn to the right hand,
and when ye turn to the left.

Isaiah 30:21

I pray the living God may be,
The shepherd of thy soul;
His tender mercies
still are free,
His mysteries to unfold.

The LORD is my shepherd;
I shall not want.

Psalm 23:1

I cannot see everything,
but nothing
escapes God.

For God shall bring every work into judgment,
with every secret thing, whether *it be* good,
or whether *it be* evil.

Ecclesiastes 12:14

A vision doesn't turn into reality without a price.

"Blessed are you when men cast insults at you, and persecute you, and say all kinds of evil against you falsely, on account of Me. "Rejoice, and be glad, for your reward in heaven is great, for so they persecuted the prophets who were before you."

Matthew 5:11-12 NASB

*The very time I
thought I was lost, my
dungeon shook and
my chains fell off.*

At midnight Paul and Silas prayed, and sang
praises unto God: and the prisoners heard them.
And suddenly there was a great earthquake,
so that the foundations of the prison were
shaken: and immediately all the doors were
opened, and every one's bands were loosed

Acts 16:25-26

Long-distance wilderness hikers have learned to set their course by a distant mountain peak rather than focus on their immediate surroundings. To reach our goals we must do the same.

Let us lay aside every weight, and the sin which doth so easily beset us, and let us run with patience the race that is set before us, Looking unto Jesus the author and finisher of our faith; who for the joy that was set before him endured the cross, despising the shame, and is set down at the right hand of the throne of God.

Hebrews 12:1-2

About the Cover Artist

Synthia Saint James, a native Californian is the designer of the award-winning U. S. Postal Stamp for Kwanzaa (1996), the first holiday stamp ever commissioned by the United States Postal Service to an African American.

In reviews her artwork has been described as "ebullient," "bold," and "joyful." One reviewer noted that she "creates paintings that remind one of the Matisse cutouts in their clear line and intense color." Her art also graces the covers of over 50 books including Terry McMillan's *Waiting to Exhale*.

She recently completed a commissioned painting, entitled "In Unity," for the International Association of Black Professional Fire Fighters (The limited edition fine art lithograph is now being sold to help raise funds for the families of the Black fire fighters lost).

She has written and/or illustrated 12 children's books. She has received a Parent's Choice Silver Honor for her book Sunday and a Coretta Scott King Honor for illustrating *Neeny Coming . . . Neeny Going*.

My art is a humbling, God-given gift, that I truly enjoy sharing.

Synthia Saint-James

References

Acknowlegements

African Proverb (6,29,30,33,43,50,53,55,69,73,
88,90,97,101,102,104,107,110,111,115,144,154),
African American Folk Saying (113), Josephine
Baker (125), Benjamin Banneker (15,21,49,
87,116), Mary McLeod Bethune (75), Bishop
Charles Blake (3,10,13,85,89,119,150,155),
Bessie Blake (54), E.W. Blyden (133), Chester
Brewer (70), L.T. Burbridge, M.D. (41), Keith
Butler (77,81,95,120,149), George Washington
Carver (20,100,127,138), Charles W. Chestnutt
(122), Honorable Shirley Chisholm (16), Rev.
G.V. Clark (106), Anna Julia Cooper (44,62,147),
Fannie Coppin (84), Joseph Cotter (57,112,128,
137), William Crogman (105), Rev. Alexander
Crummell (18,39,61,72,141), Martin Delany
(139), Frederick Douglass (5,23,34,38,66, 84,135,
143,148), W.E.B. DuBois (9,92,136), Paul
Laurence Dunbar (8,18,134,146), Marian Wright
Edelman (27), Timothy Fortune (71), Marcus
Garvey (98), Bishop Grant (65), Francis J.
Grimke (48), Jupiter Hammon (103,151),
Frances Ellen Watkins Harper (32), Bishop
Donald Hilliard (11,17,82,99), Horton (117),

John Jasper (59), Honorable Barbara Jordan (19,28), Dr. Martin Luther King (42,74,108,114), Bishop Eddie L. Long (7,36,47,132,153), Toussaint L'Ouverture (152), John Marrant (37), Benjamin Mays (123), Claude McKay (68), Kelly Miller (24), Leroy Paige (14,131), William Pickens (25,51,76,94,121), Asa Phillip Randolph (79), Honorable J.T. Settle (4), Charles W. Seymour (52), Michael Tait (80), Leroy Thompson (67,78), Albion W. Tourgee (22), Traditional Spiritual (63,118,124), Sojourner Truth (12,58,83,96,130), Harriett Tubman (64), Rev. James H. Turner (45,61), Unknown Author (31,91), William Tecumseh Vernon (26), Madam C.J. Walker (93,129), Booker T. Washington (46,56,86,142), S. E. Wesson (40), Phillis Wheatley (145), William Whipper (126), Carter Woodson (140)

Additional copies of this book and other titles
in the *God's Little Instruction Book*
series are available from your local bookstore.

If you have enjoyed this book,
or if it has impacted your life,
we would like to hear from you.

Please contact us at:

Honor books
Department E
P. O. Box 55388
Tulsa, Oklahoma 74155
Or by e-mail at info@honorbooks.com